3 A.M. Musings of Love Lost Love Found

A conscious subconscious experience of Manifestation

Chiara Atoyebi

This book is dedicated to and for all the believers. I appreciate the many that believed in this gift.

And for the one whom this book is so befitting. You entered my life with magic like words lifted from the page.

To The Moon

To the moon I say
To the moon I say
Let them have their perfection wrapped in rituals and pretty
bows
Just take me on a rocket ship to the moon
Sail me on a silhouette in soft spoken words of your
promises
Even if most of them turn up empty I will still believe them
Like the first time spoken like the last
Just a girl dyin to hear something

I heart this life
This love everlasting
This big bombastic barricade
Baby calls rollercoaster and momma calls a fool
If we throw it up in the air and it still is dangling than I know
it's true
It's hanging up there like the moon baby
Solid, bonifide…

Take me up up and away right up to the moon.

Life In An Instant

I said yes to this Life
In an Instant
With no Clues for who you Are
Just accepting we will be
And now here. We. ARE.
Two Kids
One house
A small river
And some laughter and a greater divide between us
It will take a lifetime two discover what just happened

Forget all the stuff they told you
The crazy shit is what's real
The passionate insanity
The endless debate that lies
On the brink of loyalty and letting go
Strangulation and utter devotion

If there is no pain then you are not growing
And by the looks of it we have grown exponentially
Cosmically, Spatially
Filling all gaps, holes, emptiness,
Creating and filling
Losing and finding
Until we finally stop pretending

In your eyes I saw life
When I said yes I was living

Finally no waiting
No deciding, no perfecting
No trying. The slosh pile. This hot mess.
The resting place. The remote control.
Home.
Errors, flaws, destruction, beautiful seduction
Sanity, joy and peace as we lay down to sleep.
Life in an Instant.

Laughter From The Other Side Of Heaven

From the other side of Heaven
I seek to know you
Not in this life
But next time
The next lifetime
But I need you now.

And somehow you understand me
Truthfully speaking, like no one else
I hear your whispers feel your hugs
They reach from far beyond me in this tragedy
A sunray from your spirit pierces through
Like only you can see me through this pain
I call on you quietly. Deeply to the other side.
Swiftly. Softly. Slowly. Groaning.
With pain and unknowing from the other side.
Hoping you hear me like only you can.
The other side of heaven knows no man but you
Through gripping aching, while calling forsaking
You were sent to give me comfort and I bow here in this life
And hear things from that place
You are just a whisper away
True, just, and wondrous
As I spirit dance with you.

Exhale

Like a dollar washed up on the sands
This time I love you enough to be gone till November
Sayonara my sweet love
I am still right here

I am watching you dancing
I am listening to you laughing
I am laughing too
I see you standing and speaking and being and doing
And everything and all of it and none of it
A lot of it without me and I feel every sensation
I am your heartbeat. Your every breath.

My beautiful surrender my sweet September
You are my autumn sound
Like gravy over mashed potatoes or knit socks
Who shines brighter than the sun?
Only your smile when you are in bliss
Or the Cheshire grin when you are at rest.
Run for it.

With Wings Folded

With wings folded I bow at the altar of grace
With wings folded I remember my "place"
With wings folded love encircles and surrounds my being
like
Inspiration swinging on vines and sunlight peering through
trees
And shadows grazing over the moon's light.

I used to fly
Wings wide open
Wide open outstretched and focused on the sun
Soaring high above reality
Clinging to all the things they say I should not
Knowing I had them, feeling I found them
Deep, deep within me
With wings folded

I hug myself to keep from feeling battered and bruised
I remember why I am in this life
Soaring and seeking
Forsaking and saving you daily
But mostly me
With my wings folded I enjoy a good cry
Under my feathers where no one can see but me
When no can see but me
And do and speak what no one hears or sees

That's how it feels on my knees,
Or when you are flying
Or when you growing or when you are birthing
Painful, intense, scary and necessary
Under this wing I fold.

Traditional Roles

The grin on his face curled and snapped to attention
He always liked to see her that way
Bent. Leaning

He propped her up and smiled
"In your bushes is where I belong"

He wanted action
And he kicked her leg.

She fell to her knees and cried
He wiped her tears personally
He always liked to see her that way
Bent. Leaning.

Each day they sit in a secure embrace
Leaning in. Needed.
Whispering -
"This is the job for me."

Leaves

She liked the leaves.
Rolling in them made her happy.
Cool and crunchy.
The warmth of them shielded her from the cut of cool air on
thin skin.
They covered her nakedness
in a gritty way.

Like a catcher's mit on pumpkin skins
They float, flied, scurried, shuffled to be next to her
Those leaves made her want to wiggle deeper
and feel them
She stretched out her arms like making angel wings
squinted at the sun and stuck out her tongue
Trying to catch
Something

They stuck to her body
snapped inside the cracks
left smudges and wet marks
But they covered her deep
deep
    deep
        deep
            so deep, until only her eyes showed.
Silence as she lay
Underneath the leaves

wet with tiny snowflakes
slippery with soil
safely nestled
she closed her eyes...

Leaves falling where they may.

The Last Night

I said I had no more poems in me

But since I had you in me
I had to pray to the One that sent me
He would make this sin flee

Head swirling dizzy
Like a baby
When you say go
I just go crazy
Thinking maybe
Maybe…

The shivering of my body could
Save me
Or save us
I did it because of the trust
You
The lust….

Maybe last night could rectify
What's broken

Understanding in the unspoken
Longing to be your equal
Not just a token

Last night.
The love was metaphoric
Of the category
You set for it

Loneliness.
And I can take no more of it

Heartbreak is too hard to ignore
And before you sipped my waters
You said I was what you
Thirsted for
Now I'm just your whore
Who cooks like your mother
Who you hide like your dirty laundry
And yet I come back for more.

But this is the last night…

I Hate Being Alone

I hate. I hate. I hate being alone.
When you're out I'm in
Trying not to wait by the phone

What I wouldn't give
To feel your lips
Against the soft spot
Between my hips
Lukewarm melodies you strummin' on my…
Ummmm…

I hate, I hate, I hate being alone
I hate what you turned me into
A junkie strung out on you

When I need you the most
You're not around
So I close my eyes
And fall asleep to the sounds
Of rustling covers

And I lay my head where yours should be
And a stream of tears cover my face
As I stare into the moonlight
And I imagine you walk through the door
And say I just want to hug tonight
That's the best love I get in my life
Being with you my wife

But in the meantime
Let's please each other
Love one another
I straddle you and I kiss your neck
I take the salt from my mouth
And wipe it on your chest
Arch my back
Lean forward
And let you handle the rest

When I open my eyes
I'm still staring at the moonlight
But this time it's in your eyes.

Fallen

I don't think you know what

You bring to me
Joy, pleasure, unspeakable things

I can't believe the way I've fallen
My love if only you knew
How the Sun shines brighter
When you're around
Heaven starts smiling
And angels come down
To get a glimpse of love so pure
A precious stone
An overture is heard around the world
Whenever we kiss

Without those moments my life
Would be empty.

Without those moments
My life would be empty
Without that first beat
Only found in your heart
I need yours to beat
For mine to start.

You Made Me Love You

You frighten me.
Like your easel you paint me the way you want
Me to be seen
A beautiful abstract vision with no center
No threadline. No running theme.
Just beautiful colors that sing to you
And seemingly understand everything you are going through
Look closer.
In that center lies my hidden picture
The spaces between the borders devoid of color
Therein lies my treasure.
The part of the work you missed because of its ordinariness
You focused only on the extraordinary because you fell in
love
With the picture
Not the artist.
The house
Not the foundation
Because if you would have checked
You would have seen that it was rickety
And needed more support.
Yet you make me love you.
Dominating every sense in my orifice until
I am nothing but a helpless vegetable
Subject to the ebbs and flows of your misguided affections
You squeezed my coal into I turned into your diamond

Yet I'm still rough
I still feel the sand at my temples
And you rubbing it in
I get it. I get it.
You like me…right..
Purple is my courage
But give me back my hues.
I miss my pinks, yellows and now my soul is blue
You made me love you
Like a flute you played me until I danced
And danced…
And I did. All for you.

Addicted 2 U

I'm drowning here

      Sinking fast in quicksand
          Lost in the wilderness contained in my head
             I'm too high
I wanna come down
      (I hate the come down)
I hate You.
  I really do.
      But I need you too…

You and Me

I remember turning off my television so I could listen closer
to what you were saying

I wanted to get to know you better
I wanted to admire you
I wanted to know what inspired you
I remember feeling like I didn't need to concentrate on your
past
Because we were so in the moment
The past only came up to fill in the blanks.

Instead of catching you up
It's more like, remember?
Actually, you never told me
And although I was
Half listening doing two things at once like I always do
I remember what you said
And I know it was you.

I think it's like, never wondering if it's too early or too late to
call
Cause I guess you just know I won't care

And not because you're who you think you are
But because you didn't think about it
And was just Being…And I like that.

I remember the first time I heard you laugh
And say my name slowly like you had practiced
Saying it softly in your mind over and over and over again
And it sounded good to me.

It feels like it's Here

But it's not in the way
It's far but it's still close
As if it were in my bed on the pillow next to me
Breathing hard and kissing all over my chest
Making me leave the room and sleep on the couch
Which would make me feel farther away
So I would have to go back and kiss on you too.
It's like making room
For your big shoes in my small closet
And answering my phone in the middle of my sleep
And in the middle of my session
You understanding cause we ain't got nothing but time
And me not feeling like I'm missing something because you
are
Closer than a phone call
Deeper than a letter
You're more like a rhyme with a kick ass
Bassline that's knocking so hard
I'm like forget the party
I found it in the music…your music
Sincerity is the melody
And your perseverance is the chorus
Cause your words are like the Gospel

And I receive it like scripture
And there's never any confusion
Because it's the truth.
And it sure did set me free
At least momentarily in the melody
Cause I know how it feels
to have everything and nothing
And to hear music and be caught in silence
But it's not like that
With you and me

It Feels Like

Bring back the smile
The sweet words
That flowed so effortlessly
From your lips
When you said
You wouldn't let me go

Bring back the vibration
I felt when you rubbed my feet
And I stared into your eyes
And felt myself sinking and swimming
Crying and laughing
Happy and mad
That I couldn't keep
My hands off of you
And my heart from falling

Yours eyes got me swirling
In fantasies of chocolate kisses
Honeycomb heartbreak
Hershey inspired hymnals
You strummed on my flute…
Oh, what a pleasant tune

I could pull down your lashes
And sleep on your lids
Wake up when you open your eyes
Just so we can share the same vision….

I'm trying to be on the same page

Like minded and on one accord
Finishing your sentences
Infiltrating your thoughts
Corrupting your concentration

I want you to get the shakes
If you don't get to hit
Withdrawals and cold sweats
When I withhold my kisses
Paranoia when I'm nowhere to be found
Comatose when I am.

I got you tangled in my web
Like a Black widow spider
With a pleasant smile
With a passion that hurts so good
It's borderline sadistic
And it's good to me cause it's you
And me…
It feels like spreading hot butter
Down the crack of my bun
And cookies with milk.
It's very necessary like
Breathing in and breathing out
One foot in front of the other
One leg at a time
My voice reverberating through your mind
So connected…when you think thoughts
It's my voice you hear
Lost. So lost without me.
Like the Father without the Son
Although it hurts..it has to be done
It's not about a title
This is eternal relation

And it feels like…
It *really* feels like….

Hunger. Pain.
Like Ghandi I'd make
A peaceful protest
To free this River
To quench the thirst of
Soul in need
I haven't heard you speak
But I hear you calling me
I hear you…

Mind, body and soul
Helpless you surrender
As I take control
And it feels like…
I mean it *really* feels like…

Sweet communion.

ANGEL

I got sunshine dancing at my feet

Stars that envelope my bosom
And clouds in my eyes

I am your light.

The One that shines
When you want me to dim out
I am your clock
Biologically ticking
When you want me to stop

I AM desire.

Poured over hot coals
As I rise to the surface of your subconscious
As I consciously create madness in your
Mind

Like me
You go crazy
Everytime our thoughts timelessly tango

I am your past life
We Are the future.

We are a little somethin' different
Than we both are used to

I AM you're Angel.

Time tested
Love manifested into this evolution
We've come to know
As the harmonious splendor of our fate

And not a moment too late.

LIFTED

Normally I don't like to think heavenly thoughts when I'm
on blaze

But you entered my smoke filled gaze

Illuminating the haze…

Waiting to lift me to a greater height
Now I normally like to soar somewhere in between
So I can see all around me
But you got me spinning inside your cryptic metaphors
That got me swimming
And I don't like to get wet
Better yet too wet
Cause I can't swim
But I *could* just drown in you
Or better yet
on you…
Like the buttery pats
On my pancake stack
Or like cotton sweet candy
When it lays on my tongue
Crackling and bubbling down to a sticky sweet sensation
All over my taste buds
Causing me to shiver like a hootchie at the club
Tryin' to be cute and you know she should have a coat on…

But I'm so hot in the center
I'm so hot in my center
If you push too hard
I may erupt
And if you in me
We'll combust spontaneously

I think it's written in the stars
And in your eyes
Got us flowin' so cool
Making me throw you a pound
And let you watch how I get down
I'm in possession of an illegal weapon
And I shouldn't be this high
If I keep using you I may die
Or come down…
And I don't want to
I just want you
You know?

JUS LOVE ME

My heart cries out for you

And I just cry
And I hope you see the love and sincerity in my eyes
I hope you see my hearts reflection
Deeply internalized
And it's you I choose to worship
Till the sun fails to rise
Just look in my eyes
Jus love me.

Patience

I wish I coulda been more patient.

       Jus a little more time
For you to become mine
And wander all over me
All the time
       Letting my thoughts
Intercede and bob and weave
       Through your psyche
About me
As passively as the air we breathe
       You not living without me
I, remaining one as we
Breathe just naturally

Cause you already got me
When you said
"Hey remember"
Yeah I remember
And I remember quite well
How I loved you
But be mad as hell
       Stirring in my dreams at night
You were why there was light.

       Confusion in my head

You made me not feel shady
You made me want to have your baby
And anything else you wanted me to
I just wanted you
With the same
         Selfishly, sick, urgent way
You had me on top of you
On top of me
Telling me
What you were telling me.
I know sincerity.

So let's stop frontin'
We are the one each other's wantin'
Don't think I'm crazy
Or could hurt you
Show me how to trust you
Jus what is this love worth to you?

Searching

Why you want to send me in circles?
You said you were honest.

While we were steady spooning
Sending our slow grinds into sensations
I couldn't separate love from your extension
Searching for answers in your smiles
Affirmations in your eyes
Somethin' that you were feeling me too
Cuz I am sure feeling you.

I know it's just emotions
But my emotions got the best of me
And I can't separate love from the game
Searching for inflections in your voice
When you say my name
When you say my name
I mean, if you say my name
Just say something…

You say call me Daddy, cause I'm your good girl.
But my mind is spinning, sliding from your separation
From my sanity,
Swirling my joy into isolation.
And it's like madness.
I mean, it's so supposed to hurt so good
But this just hurts.

You got us loving and growing in spurts.
Back and forth asking
What is it all worth?

Ten minutes of a connection
And when you bless my body
I feel this resurrection
Spiraling into a Milky Way of ecstasy
I paid the price of my soul to have you next to me
Good or bad
This is my destiny.

And I don't hesitate to participate in this love hate.
Maybe I'm just searching
Like 2/3 steady trying to become whole
But like flour I fail to rise
Especially with the weight of you on my mind
Stifling my progress
And when you kiss me I just digress
Cuz without you I can't see.

What real love can be like without sweet misery.
Then you look into my eyes and kiss me gently
Right at the moment I was feeling empty.
That was all I was searching for.

Breaking the Cycle

I got one shot and two second chances

I don't get three or I'm struck out—
Sideturned and sidetracked
Turned out and setback,
To where I first left my confusion.

I got a deeper meaning under this smile
More like broken glass
Shattered by the butt of a smoking gun
I shot myself with…time and time again..

I got one shot
And I steady, aimed, and shot it at you
To preserve me—
Cause I want off this track
And you keep sidetracking me…

So I trip and play mind tricks
And my heart bleeds
I contemplate, I fixate, and I obsess about things
I try, I get high, and I don't know what I perceive
I fall flat I bounce back
I scream don't abandon Me.

Cause with no love I can't breathe
With too much I can't see
In the middle I'm losing me
Knockin' on doors
Twisting locks with the wrong key
My mind is menacing it plays tricks on me
And brings you into my world

Secret Affair

The secret walk
The forbidden dance
We lock our eyes
And you put me in your trance.

The moon shined bright
As we danced the night away
Secretly minds intertwined
On that fateful Wednesday.

Naked we lay as
We watched the sunrise
But the real magic was
Caught in your eyes.

Thinking back burns a
Fever between my thighs
And your mind, to it
Constantly alluding
Making your nature rise,
Like the sun we set as we
Mesh and become one flesh

The secret code of mysteries untold
Between two lovers
That never touched each other
Yet love one another…secretly.

A Crazy Dream

As I travel down the hall
I notice pictures of butterflies and roses
Farmers with hoses
But one caught my eye with these fixtures
Dark, gloomy, cold were the eyes
The mood got a hold
The grip was so bold
In my heart, in my mind
I tried to run but only swayed
The eyes bore into me and stayed
I longed to go
I longed to leave
Those dark gloomy eyes kept taunting me
It came to me in an epiphany
It was he from my dream
I opened my arms please let me in
Together my love lets ride the wind
To a place where only you and I dwell
Those eyes they stare at me
I'm scared as hell
This longing this love
This fire burns deep
This passion, this pain, the soles of my feet
Will run to you and bond our souls
My heart you can have
I want to be loved
Spirit on top of spirit exchanging fantastically orgasmic
spiritual emotions
This is how I want you to love me
With your eyes and mind

They hold the key
Unfolding a secret love that is predestined to be
So I will run to you my beautiful picture
Corrupted mesmerizing scandalous fixture
I've painted you all my life in my mind
Now you are mine
Consecrated in my heart until the end of the next
Lifetime.

YOU WANT PEACE

My words be glorified
As I manifest complete
Sunshine so blinding
Their eyes can't take my heat
This is how it looks when the light speaks.

Thunder clashes when my heart beats
Firmament moves these mountains cause I'm free
It's the light in me
My wordplay sets the captives free
I hear my name being whispered
For the God in me
I rise to the call cause I am He

Soul linked from the creator
I create cause we are We
Like image spirit similar
The trinity abides in me
Flow waters eternal
Linking our destinies.

You want peace
Rest in me

Day by Day

I find truth
In your reflection
When I pray.

I sacrifice my soul
Come naked
Give me your pain

I can take it
The sacrificial lamb
Don't mistake this.
Don't miss this power
Placed before your feet
On my knees
Wisdom taps my shoulder
Knowledge opens to me
The longer I honor
The more that's given me
My mind is the architect
Destiny succumbs to me
I cherish Love and it makes me queen
What I visualize is what I bring

Day by Day
Resistance I slay
Placing all burdens at sevens gate
White horses and magistrates
Sound trumpets for our names
Recouping what was stolen
Reviling another soldier slain
We do it for love
We do it for his name
We do it to heal sorrow
We do it to end pain
We do it for the order we maintain.
1000 years is over justice now rains.

Grab your crowns and hold them high
For the recovery of the blinded eye
We are the light.

3 A.M.

The happy girl. The smiling girl.
The happy girl. The smiling girl.
The sad girl. The lonely girl.
The sad girl. The mad girl.
In her own world.

She is awakened by the dull thud of silence
Ringing in her ears.
Stares into the mirror until she cries.

Lonely girl.
In a state of confusion
Rises out of bed wandering
Aimlessly towards nothing
Trips over the clock
It's 3 a.m.
Too early. Too late.

Her mate. Insipid.
Shifts in his sleep
She calls his name in the night
An inaudible whisper
Resonating in her head like a crescendo.
Sad girl. Lonely girl.

She drags the radio into the bathroom
Lays on the floor pressed to the speaker
Feeding off the words and melodies
Needing the interaction like hope
Desperate to break the silence.
Lonely girl. Desperate girl.

It's not enough.
She jumps up and grabs her car keys
She has to get out of here
Turn off the radio.
Check house.
Mate still insipid.
House still.
Silence impenetrable.

She prepares for a trip to nowhere
Headed towards nothing
Her mental state paralyzes her
She slams the keys on the floor
Silence impenetrable
Mate still insipid.
She kicks the table breaking the glass
She needs some noise. Some energy.
(crazy girl)
She's free now.
To maintain this sanity
She allows her self to go insane
To feel the disorder.

She strips her clothing
Smears her perspiration
Straight faced intense
She holds her weapon in hand
She's got to help her situation.

She writes the names of her demons
All over her body.
Hate, pain, desperation, fear.
Just go. She writes…
One lone tear falls from her eye

With the pen
Hitting the floor at the same time.

She catches her reflection in the mirror.
Who was that?
Crazy girl. Crazy girl.

She looks at herself from a faraway place
Inside her body
She is surprised. Who was that?
Disgusted girl. Confused girl.

Check the house. Mate insipid.
House quiet. Radio off.
She slips into bed.
Mate awakes in time to use her and sleep again.
In the morning she awakens.
Happy girl. Happy girl.

Happy. Normal.
House the same.
Mate awake smiling.
Last night forgotten committed by a peculiar possession
Of pestilence.

The only reminder were the words written
On her body reminding her of her nighttime visitation
At 3 a.m.

VICTIM OF THE GAME

I'm tired of being strong
Tired of carrying your weight
Making it mine
You say it's ours- you would do the same
But the only one carrying is me
Victim of the game.

What we say we would not do
Are the things we do the most
As we allow our bodies to become the parasite's host
On my sympathy you play
My smiling face makes me easy prey
I'm the one to blame
Victim of the game.

What are the benefits if I lay down with you?
Unlock my virtue unto you
Only to allow a stronger hold on me
Through all the screams
And packed bags at the door
You see through to my weakness
Revealing me your emotional whore
Coming and going with you is a spiritual war
All you want to do is love me
Until I can't take no more.

If you love somebody
Set them free
But how can they go
If they refuse to let
This tug of war is killing me
Victim of the game.

I Was Made Love To

I was made love to

Even if he didn't know me
And I knew it was love
Because we danced so simply.

I was made love to
In the still of the night
No elaborate candles
Our bodies radiated the light.

I was made love to
No fake moanin'
Just blended teardrops and
Harmonious breathing
Elevated the moment.
Something else must have been in the room
Orchestrating the union
My body did pirouettes
And there was no confusion
The touch like fire
The crashing waves
The slow, steady, love we made.
(If only for one night I was saved)
Cause I was made love to
Who knows if he loved me
But it was honest lovemaking
And he dances beautifully.

How could it be that

The magic is gone?
Was hypnotized in a trance
With a wave of your wand
Now a heart box filled with dreams
And my vision of truth
And in that vision there is no you.

Somewhere on the interstate
I lost my youth
Scars on my heart bare proof.

Looking for a laugh
Searching for a place to take me back
Oh, let me regain
The confidence when I say my name
The courage to blaze the earth like a flame

Strangely, amaze me
Evident I see
I feel scorched earth
Where passion should be
Rain, sweet rain, rain down on me.

A weeping willow grows in place
Of my flower
As time, waits for no one
Diminishing my power.
How on earth could we ignore?
The sign on the wall

KARAMEL MOCHA

It's just one of those moments
When I think of you,
Eyes as dark as Onyx
Deep set, intense.

A line makes its way across
Your forehead and dances
On your face
Eyes truly are the light to the soul.

You look like a boy with a man's eyes
The prodigal Son, the Chosen One.
Life has made your mind hard
But your heart remains soft.

My sweet, sweet baby
I love the way you look at me
I love the way you say my name.
You don't have to say a word
It's all in how you kiss me.

Lips so soft and warm
Lookin' at me through thick lashes
My heart pounds
I'm drunk in your presence
Your aura is hypnotizing
Your emotion is making me sway

Caress me sugar
Love me daddy
With you I want to make it right

Talk about Love Jones
You got my soul
I'm like
Water flowin' with you
The leaves blowin' with you
You are like the sunshine in the mist
Of my storm…

A protector a provider
All that..
And you haven't even said a word.

I hear your voice in my head
You know all my thoughts
You lived them.

You know all the answers to my questions
You wrote them.

Valor, sexiness, strength
But most of all love
Describes you
I don't mean that silly love
Cause love can be oh so silly

I'm mean that better than sex love
That better than weed love
That better than a call in the midnight hour love
That…
I-got-you-open-what-you-smokin'-I'm-so-drunk-I-feel-you-
baby
Love, Love, Love
Oh my sweet love…

So why don't you slowly
Lay me down
In the bath water
And trace your name across my back
Cause I am yours
My Karamel Mocha.

Feel Free

You make me feel free.

You make me feel like
Cold lemonade on a hot day
Black coffee for my hangover
A foot rub for my feet
You spell relief.

You make me feel free.

Like I'm relaxing in a hammock
And sleeping under a breeze
Like I can speak from my heart
And not have to think
Got me feelin' faded
Every time our eyes meet
I see your life lessons
And they're mirroring me.

You make me feel free.

My Body's Not Your Playgound

Mind meandering

Lost
Concave introspections
Resolute connections
I reach for the sky
Then bless them.

Focused on the rebirth
Focused on this work
You focused on my self-worth
And I fight to keep my esteem high

My body's not ur playground
Mind wavering
Stolen like my virtue
Found like my sensitivity
Syncopated rhyme tones
When you touch me tenderly
You say you feeling blessed
I say cause Heaven sent me
And when I resist your strong holds
You start to resent me.

Why you gotta posses me?
Mind, body and soul
The way your love ingests me
Demanding total control.

Well my body's not UR playground
My ass is not your tree

Stop hanging 'round my branches
Unless you're sowing seed
Stop trying to eat my apples
And lay up under me.

Ethereal, they call my name
'Cause I'm eternally free
Yet you try to eat my apples
That's just not my destiny
That's just not my destiny.

Spread Your Wings And Dream

Did you know you had invisible wings
Predestined to soar?

To places on this Earth
In this lifetime
Serenity you will find
But it first starts in the mind

The question is not
What He can give you
But what you can believe
The quiet in the mist of the storm
The silence with
The caress of the breeze

What you want
And what He can do
Is far more than you could ever dream

No one in this life
Is meant to be with none
But you speak what you are
With the power of the tongue

A dream deferred is as strong as death
And if a man has no dreams
He has nothing left
This world will choke him

Those binding chains
And snatch his dreams
Until he's no longer the same
Tell him his kids don't need him
Unless he comes with a lot of change
But to a child
Attention from Momma is just the same

They say a man is washed up
When he can no longer run with the ball
So he stays out late
Turns to alcohol
But don't give up so easy
Don't try to mask your pain
Because the prayers of the righteous
Can stop the Rain

You've been a doctor all your life
You decide no more
You realize your house
Lavish lifestyle
May come crumbling to the floor
But that's the chance
You have to take
In order to make the music
Your soul called you to make for when a
talent is buried
How can it breathe?
If it's not given life
And a chance to achieve

How can you be
All that you are created to be
Until the veil is lifted

And blind eyes made to see
If you don't see
Who will see?
That you are
Who you said you would be

That your dreams really are
Your reality
Starting first with the dream
The vision and plan carried out to a tee

Fathers, achievers, dream seekers,
believers
Brothers, friends, sons of men
If you don't see
Who will see
That you can be all that you believe?

It takes just a moment to do the most
courageous thing
To think the thought
To dream the dream
More courageous than anything
So look towards heaven and spread your
wings and dream

www.ingramcontent.com/pod-product-compliance
Lightning Source LLC
Chambersburg PA
CBHW060618030426
42337CB00018B/3109